World Wonders 3

John Chapman

NATIONAL GEOGRAPHIC LEARNING | CENGAGE Learning

Australia • Brazil • Japan • Korea • Mexico • Singapore • Spain • United Kingdom • United States

World Wonders 3 Test Book

John Chapman

Publisher: Jason Mann

Director of Content Development: Sarah Bideleux

Managing Editor: Angela Cussons

Associate Development Editor: Phillip McElmuray

Art Director/Cover Designer: Natasa Arsenidou

Text Designer/Compositor: Dora Danasi

National Geographic Editorial Liaison:
Leila Hishmeh

ISBN: 978-1-4240-7890-5

National Geographic Learning
Cheriton House, North Way, Andover, Hampshire, SP10 5BE
United Kingdom

Cengage Learning is a leading provider of customized learning solutions with office locations around the globe, including Singapore, the United Kingdom, Australia, Mexico, Brazil and Japan. Locate your local office at: **international.cengage.com/region**

Cengage Learning products are represented in Canada by Nelson Education, Ltd.

Visit National Geographic Learning online at **ngl.cengage.com**

Visit our corporate website at **www.cengage.com**

Photo credits

Anthony Stewart/National Geographic Image Collection, Peter Essick/National Geographic Image Collection, Chris Newbert/Minden Pictures/National Geographic Image Collection, Jim Richardson/National Geographic Image Collection, Alaska Stock Images/National Geographic Image Collection, Carsten Peter/National Geographic Image Collection, Richard Nowitz/National Geographic Image Collection, Il Kwon/Your Shot National Geographic Image Collection, Massimo Bassano/National Geographic Image Collection, Patrick McFeeley/National Geographic Image Collection, Bill Curtsinger/National Geographic Image Collection, Michael Nichols/National Geographic Image Collection, Greg Ludwig/National Geographic Image Collection, Flip Nicklin/National Geographic Image Collection

Printed in the United Kingdom by Lightning Source
Print Number 07 Print Year 2018

Contents

Score Sheet

Test 1   / 50

Test 2   / 50

Test 3   / 50

Test 4   / 50

Test 5   / 50

Test 6   / 50

Mid-Year Test   / 80

Test 7   / 50

Test 8   / 50

Test 9   / 50

Test 10   / 50

Test 11   / 50

Test 12   / 50

End-of-Year Test   / 80

Test 1

⭐ Fascinating Places

Vocabulary

A Write the missing letters.

1 This means many thousands of years old.   p _ _ _ _ _ _ _ _ _ _
2 This work of art is sometimes made of stone.   s _ _ _ _ _ _ _ _ _
3 You can buy many different kinds of things in this place.   m _ _ _ _ _ _
4 This is a line between two countries.   b _ _ _ _ _ _
5 This uses water and you can see one in a public square.   f _ _ _ _ _ _ _ _   / 5

B Circle the correct words.

1 The river is very shallow / powerful. You can even walk across it.
2 The queen of England lives in an impressive palace / tunnel.
3 The bridge / temple is 400 years old, but you can still drive over it.
4 There is a rocky / huge stone monument in the town centre.
5 The Greek islands have got many sandy / steep beaches.   / 5

C Complete the sentences with these adjectives.

| bare   deep   flat   muddy   narrow |

1 The area where I live is very _____, so walking is easy.
2 The campsite is _____ because it rained all day yesterday.
3 The Grand Canyon is nearly two kilometres _____ in some places.
4 This small island is _____ . It hasn't got any trees or plants.
5 You can't drive in this part of town. The streets are very _____ .   / 5

D Choose the correct answers.

1 Mark and Julie set _____ on their trip at 7 am.
  a in   b up   c off
2 Michael and Fran went _____ for the weekend.
  a on   b away   c over
3 Leslie and Steve checked _____ early for their flight.
  a in   b out   c into
4 The family's car broke _____ during their road trip.
  a off   b into   c down
5 Mr and Mrs Hobbs got _____ the bus just before it left.
  a over   b up   c on   / 5

Grammar

A Complete the sentences using the Present Simple or the Present Continuous of the verbs in brackets.

1 Peter _____ (take) photographs of his friends right now.
2 Rachel always _____ (buy) souvenirs for her friends.
3 She _____ (stay) with her aunt and uncle this weekend.
4 The people in this photograph _____ (smile).
5 The bus to Cardiff _____ (leave) at 5 o'clock every afternoon.

/ 5

B Complete the sentences with these verbs using the Present Simple or the Present Continuous.

> hate   meet   not own   remember   stay

1 Lisa _____ the weather in England, so she's moving to Italy.
2 I _____ Paul for coffee near the Eiffel Tower.
3 _____ James _____ in England at the moment?
4 I _____ this place from the picture on the postcard.
5 Brian's parents _____ a house in the Canary Islands.

/ 5

C Circle the correct words.

1 'What are you thinking / do you think of the mountain?' 'It's really amazing.'
2 Jessica sees / is seeing a person in a travel company today about her trip.
3 'This house is the oldest one in the village.' 'Oh, I see / think.'
4 Jeff thinks / is thinking about driving across the country this summer.
5 'I see / am seeing you know a lot about Peru.' 'Yes, I go there often.'

/ 5

D Complete the sentences with who, whose, which, where or when.

1 Is that the woman _____ house is on a mountain?
2 A temple is a place _____ it's often very quiet.
3 My uncle, _____ is a pilot, has travelled to 20 countries.
4 The guides don't give tours of the castle grounds _____ it rains.
5 Let's stay in a place _____ has got a nice view of the beach.

/ 5

Reading

A Read this advertisement for a rafting trip.

See the Grand Canyon on a Rafting Trip

Join us for our exciting rides on the Colorado River!
Our rafting adventures take you to the most beautiful parts
of the Grand Canyon. Don't just stand and look at the canyon
– be a part of an adventure!

Lee's Ferry Rafting Adventures has got three-day trips and
seven-day trips available. Our trips include camping at
campsites along the river, stops for meals as you travel,
and hiking trips to places which you can only reach from the
river. Some of the things you'll enjoy include:

- **fascinating views from inside the Grand Canyon;**
- **the Bridge of Sighs, a massive natural stone bridge;**
- **the beautiful blue-green waters of Havasu Creek;**
- **ancient monuments and traditional Native American homes;**
- **many exciting rapids and impressive rock formations.**

You can trust that our rafting equipment will keep you
safe. All of our rafts are over 10 metres long and we make
sure everyone wears a life jacket. We've been in business
since 1975 and all of our guides have at least five years'
experience. For safety reasons, we don't allow children
under 12 years old on the trips.

Call 1-888-348-7990 for more details.

Comprehension

B Write R (Right), W (Wrong) or DS (Doesn't say).

1 The rafting company offers week-long trips.

2 You can't do any hiking while on the trips.

3 The Bridge of Sighs is a modern bridge.

4 The Native Americans give tours of their homes.

5 Small children can't go on the trips.

 / 10

 Total / 50

Test 2

Amazing Science

Vocabulary

A Put the letters in the correct order to find sizes.

1 s s m v i a e   _____
2 m l l a s   _____
3 u g h e   _____
4 y t n i   _____
5 m o o n r e u s   _____

◯ / 5

B Complete the sentences with make or do.

1 We often _____ mistakes when we're in a hurry.
2 Scientists _____ a lot of research for their projects.
3 The children _____ their homework at 8 o'clock every night.
4 Can you please _____ a decision – yes or no?
5 Many new inventions _____ a big difference in our lives.

◯ / 5

C Choose the correct answers.

1 A solar oven can help _____ money and energy.
  a spend
  b save
  c weigh

2 Astronomers usually work in _____ .
  a observatories
  b telescopes
  c rockets

3 We use _____ when we talk about temperatures.
  a degrees
  b rays
  c kilometres

4 We can see the moon at night because it _____ light from the sun.
  a follows
  b creates
  c reflects

5 The Earth is the only _____ that people can live on.
  a star
  b planet
  c universe

◯ / 5

D Circle the correct words.

1 The scientist congratulated the team with / on their work.
2 Astronauts have to deal with / for many problems in their job.
3 Many scientists concentrate in / on discovering new life forms.
4 Astronomers are always searching for / with new objects in space.
5 Will humans succeed on / in living on the moon?

◯ / 5

Grammar

A Complete the sentences with these verbs using the Past Simple or the Past Continuous.

> buy   fall   not study   see   write

1 Mike was running to the observatory when he _____ .
2 I _____ a new computer last week with the money that Dad gave me.
3 Carla _____ for her science test when I called at her house.
4 We _____ a scary alien movie in the cinema yesterday afternoon.
5 _____ you _____ an email to Robert when I called you?

◯ / 5

B Complete the dialogue using the Present Perfect Simple or the Past Simple of the verbs in brackets.

Lee: (1) _____ you _____ (visit) the new space museum yet, David?

David: No, I haven't. I (2) _____ (hear) George talking about it yesterday, though.

Lee: It's brillant. Why don't you go?

David: I (3) _____ (want) to go last week, but I (4) _____ (have) a lot of homework recently.

Lee: Me too. But I (5) _____ (go) on Wednesday to see the Mars exhibition. It was the last day of it! The rest of the museum was great too.

◯ / 5

C Choose the correct answers.

1 Omar _____ to be an astronaut.
   a used to   b didn't use   c did use
2 'Is Tracy at home?' 'No, she's _____ to her astronomy class.'
   a been   b went   c gone
3 Bill _____ a lot of science books when he was a child.
   a has read   b used to read   c was reading
4 '_____ to the new science exhibition yet?' 'No, I'm going with Josh tomorrow.'
   a Have you been   b Did you go   c Have you gone
5 Michael has worked on the space programme _____ .
   a in 2004   b all day yesterday   c for two years

◯ / 5

D Write sentences or questions using these words. Use the Present Perfect Simple or the Past Simple.

1 scientists / not find / intelligent life / yet

_____

2 ? / you / visit / the observatory / already

_____

3 the astromoner / discover / a new planet / in 2002

_____

4 ? / you / never see / a star / through a telescope

_____

5 people / already try / to contact aliens

_____

◯ / 5

Reading

A Read this dialogue between a maths teacher and his student.

Anna:	Mr Miller, how long have calculators been around?
Mr Miller:	A very long time, Anna. The first kind of calculator was invented in China in the 800s and it was called an 'abacus'. It was made of wood and it didn't use electricity at all.
Anna:	I see. How did it work?
Mr Miller:	An abacus has got many round pieces of wood. You move them from one place to another, and this is how you use an abacus to count.
Anna:	Hmm, it sounds a bit difficult to use.
Mr Miller:	Yes, but people used them to count for years. Then, a mathematician named Pascal invented a new kind of calculator in the 1600s. It looked like a large metal box with wheels inside.
Anna:	That sounds really different from my calculator.
Mr Miller:	It was. Pascal's calculator was very big and heavy. Then, in the 1880s a man named William Burroughs invented a more modern calculator. It was expensive, but a lot of businesses used it.
Anna:	Did that calculator use electricity?
Mr Miller:	No, it didn't. In fact, the first small electrical calculators weren't made until 1966. They were very light.
Anna:	Oh, so they were like mine?
Mr Miller:	Not exactly, and they were a lot more expensive back then.
Anna:	Well, I really depend on mine. And I think it's great that it uses solar power. That way, I don't have to change the batteries!

Comprehension

B Answer the questions.

1 Where was the first calculator invented?

_____

2 What did Pascal's calculator have inside it?

_____

3 When did Burroughs invent his calculator?

_____

4 What were the first small electrical calculators like?

_____ ⬭ / 10

5 Why does Anna like her calculator?

_____

Total ⬭ / 50

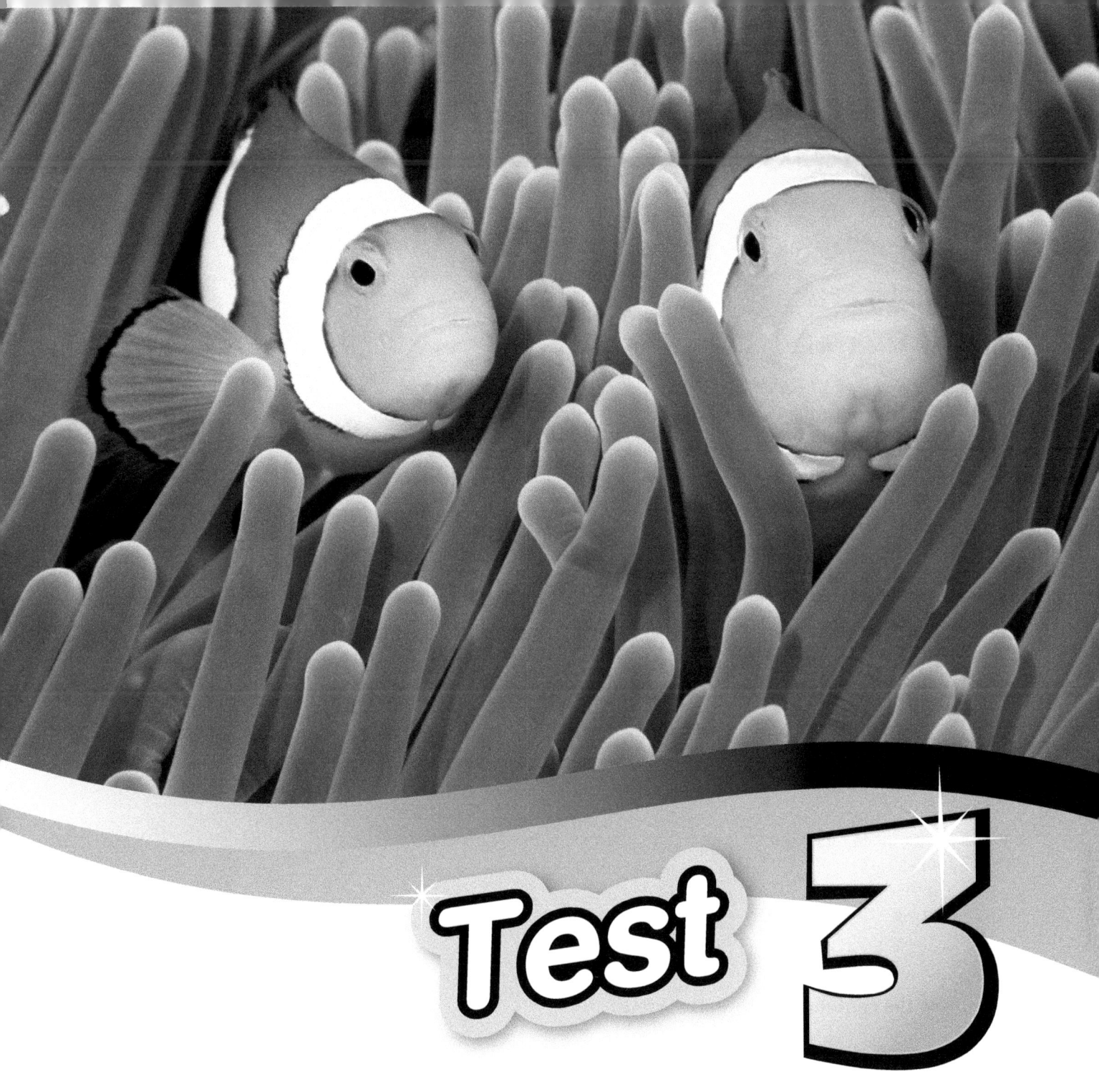

Test 3

3 The Natural World

Vocabulary

A Circle the correct words.

1 The storm / volcano sent smoke a mile into the sky.
2 The bird held onto the tree branch with its claws / horns.
3 Can scientists estimate / encourage how big the dinosaurs were?
4 What special appearance / equipment do you need to study the weather?
5 An animal's bone / fur keeps it warm in winter.

/ 5

B Choose the correct answers.

1 The heavy rain caused a terrible _____ .
  a drought
  b flood
  c wildfire

2 Louis used a(n) _____ to chop the wood.
  a beak
  b shovel
  c axe

3 All of the dinosaurs were _____ .
  a snakes
  b lizards
  c reptiles

4 The fish had very colourful _____ .
  a paws
  b wings
  c scales

5 Opening times for the nature park are listed on the _____ .
  a motto
  b evidence
  c leaflet

/ 5

C Complete the sentences with these words.

> build   cause   give   put   spread

1 How many firemen did it take to _____ out the large fire?
2 An earthquake can _____ a lot of damage to an area.
3 We _____ out information to people who visit the centre.
4 The company wants to _____ a hotel next to the forest.
5 Did the fire _____ to other buildings?

/ 5

D Match.

1 Dinosaurs died
2 We all have to cut
3 Scientists are looking
4 Neil tried to get
5 Do you think the world will ever run

a down on the amount of electricity we use.
b across to his sister how important saving energy is.
c out of energy?
d into the use of new energy sources.
e out thousands of years ago.

/ 5

Grammar

A Complete the sentences with these words using the Present Perfect Continuous.

do   encourage   not recycle   read   take

1 They _____ people to save energy for years.
2 I _____ the bus to work lately.
3 _____ you _____ research on pollution for a long time?
4 Jill _____ books on environmental problems all week.
5 Our neighbours _____ any of their rubbish recently.

/ 5

B Complete the paragraphs using the Present Perfect Simple or the Present Perfect Continuous of the verbs in brackets.

Earthquakes are very dangerous natural disasters. They happen in some parts of the world more than others. In California, massive earthquakes (1) _____ (happen) for millions of years. Most people who live in this area (2) _____ (feel) a strong earthquake at least once in their life. Although many people (3) _____ (die) in past earthquakes, it's not as dangerous as it seems. The number of people living in the state (4) _____ (grow) quickly for many years.

Scientists (5) _____ (study) earthquakes for a long time. They (6) _____ (discover) many things about them already, such as what causes them and what happens under the ground. People (7) _____ (make) changes to the way they build things since the 1960s. They (8) _____ (build) skyscrapers, bridges, and even tunnels that can survive strong earthquakes, and these changes (9) _____ (save) many lives. This (10) _____ (encourage) people who live in other places that have earthquakes to change the way they build things too.

/ 10

C The words in bold are wrong. Write the correct words.

1 Scientists recently discovered the **large** fossil in the world.   _____
2 Hurricanes are more powerful **by** ordinary storms.   _____
3 Michael thinks dinosaurs are **most** interesting than birds.   _____
4 This year's wildfire spread **quick** than the one two years ago.   _____
5 I think earthquakes are the **bad** natural disaster.   _____

/ 5

Reading

A Read the article about Mount St Helens.

Mount St Helens is a huge volcano in the state of Washington, USA. For many years people called it the Mount Fuji of America because it looked like the famous Japanese mountain. Native Americans who lived near the volcano told stories about its natural beauty for hundreds of years. The area had impressive forests, a beautiful lake and many country homes.

For years Mount St Helens seemed just like a quiet snowy mountain, but on 16 March 1980 the mountain began to change. There were lots of small earthquakes and the shape of the enormous mountain began to change. It was no longer safe to stay in the area.

Some people living near the volcano didn't want to leave, though. They didn't believe that there was any danger. Then on 18 May 1980 there was a powerful earthquake and the massive top of the mountain exploded. Hot rock from the volcano caused wildfires, burning thousands of trees. People who were still in the area tried to leave, but in the end 57 people died.

In recent years the volcano has become quiet, but a little smoke still rises from its centre. Scientists are watching the volcano closely because they want to avoid the kind of disaster it caused in 1980.

Comprehension

B Circle the correct words.

1 Mount St Helens is a volcano in Japan / Washington.

2 Native Americans used to write / talk about its beauty.

3 The mountain began to change before / after the powerful earthquake.

4 Wildfires burned thousands of people / trees.

5 There is still hot rock / smoke coming from the volcano.

/ 10

Total  / 50

Test 4

4 Myths and Legends

Vocabulary

A Match.

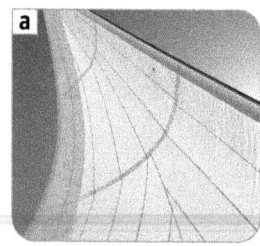 a
 b
 c
 d
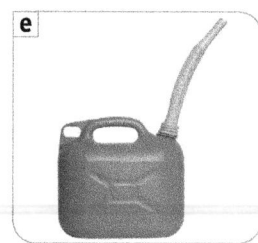 e

1 sword ☐   4 labyrinth ☐
2 bull ☐   5 sail ☐
3 fuel ☐

/ 5

B Choose the correct answers.

1 He gave me €100 for my birthday. He's _____ .
   a impatient   b responsible   c generous

2 Tom was _____ because he was sick for ten days.
   a wise   b miserable   c cheerful

3 Macy's dad can lift heavy boxes. He's quite _____ .
   a strong   b careless   c cowardly

4 The weather was _____ yesterday. It rained all day.
   a weak   b unpleasant   c mean

5 Tom asked Wendy to be _____ and wait for a few minutes.
   a brave   b unkind   c patient

/ 5

C Circle the correct words.

1 I hope I get a chance / surprise to see a UFO some day.
2 Alexander got a job / reply as a tour guide.
3 The legend / war says that giants once lived in the area.
4 The plane crashed / took off into the sea, but everyone survived.
5 After travelling for hours, they finally arrived / landed at the castle.

/ 5

D Complete the sentences with these words.

afraid   capable   interested   suitable   worried

1 Ancient Greek boats were _____ of travelling long distances.
2 Is John _____ about flying tomorrow?
3 Very windy weather isn't _____ for flying.
4 Mona is _____ in learning about world mythology.
5 Lisa is _____ of high places.

/ 5

Grammar

A Write sentences or questions using these words. Use the Past Perfect Simple.

1 a few students / already visit / Crete

_____

2 they / hear / about the mystery / before their trip

_____

3 Jake / never read / about Stonehenge

_____

4 ? / Amelia Earhart / fly / across the Atlantic / by 1932

_____

5 Mandy / not study / ancient myths / before the age of ten

_____

/ 5

B Write short answers.

1 Had Mike seen the UFO movie before tonight? _____ (✓)
2 Had you and your mum already heard about the legend? _____ (✓)
3 Had Mike and Tracy flown in a small plane before? _____ (✗)
4 Had they ever seen strange lights in the sky? _____ (✓)
5 Had the city disappeared by 700? _____ (✗)

/ 5

C Circle the correct words.

Last summer, my uncle Bill (1) visited / had visited Scotland. He (2) didn't visit / hadn't visited the country before. He (3) wanted / had wanted to see as much of it as he could. Uncle Bill (4) read / had read several stories about the Loch Ness monster before the trip, and he (5) hoped / had hoped to see this legend with his own eyes while he was there. When he (6) arrived / had arrived in Scotland he immediately headed for Loch Ness. When he got there, he (7) rented / had rented a boat and began sailing around the lake. After he (8) was / had been on the water for about an hour, he suddenly saw something very strange about 100 metres from his boat. It (9) was / had been about 8 metres long and it was moving very fast, but he couldn't see it very clearly. Was it the Loch Ness monster or not? He was certain that he (10) saw / had seen something, but he wasn't sure what it was. He'll probably never know for sure.

/ 10

Reading

A Read this legend about the Giant's Causeway.

Legend has it that a long time ago, an Irish giant named Finn MacCool lived in northern Ireland. MacCool lived near the sea of Moyle and across the sea was Scotland, where a giant called Benandonner lived. Benandonner was Finn's greatest enemy. He was the only other giant as big as MacCool.

The two giants had never met, but MacCool decided that he wanted to fight Benandonner. The fight would show which giant was the strongest. There wasn't a boat big enough to carry giants, so MacCool built a causeway of huge stones. That way, MacCool could walk to Scotland and fight Benandonner.

However, as MacCool got closer to Scotland, he saw Benandonner and became afraid of his size. The Scottish giant was much bigger and more unpleasant than MacCool had realised. When Benandonner saw him, he started to run after him. MacCool ran to his home and asked his wife what to do. She put a baby's dress on him and put him in a big baby's bed. When Benandonner arrived, MacCool's wife asked him not to wake up the baby. She told Benandonner that the baby was MacCool's child. Benandonner immediately ran away. If this giant baby was the child of MacCool, Benandonner didn't want to meet MacCool, so Benandonner ran all the way back to Scotland on the Giant's Causeway.

Comprehension

B Answer the questions.

1 Who lived in Scotland?

_____

2 Which giant decided he wanted to fight with the other?

_____

3 What made MacCool scared of Benandonner?

_____

4 What did MacCool's wife put on him when he came home?

_____

5 How did Benandonner get back to Scotland?

_____

/ 10

Total / 50

Test 5

Vocabulary

A Write the missing letters.

1 This is a job that a person does for many years.   c _ _ _ _ _ _
2 This is someone who does very bad things.   c _ _ _ _ _ _ _ _
3 This describes someone who makes a lot of money.   w _ _ _ - _ _ _ _
4 This describes someone who wants to be successful.   a _ _ _ _ _ _ _ _
5 This is someone who tries to keep people safe.   p _ _ _ _ _ o _ _ _ _ _ _   **/ 5**

B Choose the correct answers.

1 Kim got her _____ from Oxford.
   a degree
   b course
   c occupation

2 He wants to start his own _____ in less than a year.
   a interview
   b business
   c training

3 Nancy asked her _____ for a pay rise.
   a boss
   b worker
   c writer

4 Neil hopes to have a large _____ one day.
   a salary
   b application
   c qualification

5 What _____ do you need for this job?
   a adverts
   b skills
   c professions

/ 5

C Circle the correct words.

1 The weather is always sensible / damp in a rainforest.
2 Rick slept in a hammock / mosquito net that he made out of rope.
3 Choosing a career can be a really tough / spare decision.
4 Mark has over 3,000 songs on his MP3 player / GPS unit.
5 Paul caught dinner for everyone with his new first aid kit / fishing rod.

/ 5

D The words in bold are wrong. Write the correct words.

1 Mary turned **off** the invitation to go climbing. She was too busy to go.   _____
2 They can't keep **down** with the other people in the group.   _____
3 Tom can't get **under** how good his brother is at football.   _____
4 How can you put **over** with this terrible heat?   _____
5 I'm not going to give **down**. I will try harder.   _____

/ 5

Grammar

A Choose the correct answers.

1 There _____ be a training programme for employees.
   a going to   b will   c isn't going
2 The courses _____ on Friday mornings.
   a will to be   b will be   c is going to be
3 I probably _____ attend that university.
   a am not   b won't   c aren't going to
4 Are you _____ climb that high mountain?
   a going to   b will   c going
5 No, I _____ going to travel the world just yet.
   a won't   b 'm not   c 'll not

/ 5

B Circle the correct words.

Bob: I have decided that I (1) will / am going to study for the Spanish test all week.

Mary: That's impressive, Bob!

Bob: If you want, I (2) will / am going to help you with your studies, too.

Mary: Have you decided if you (3) will / are going to use the listening tapes?

Bob: Yes, of course. It's good to use them.

Mary: Do you think the test (4) is going to / will be hard?

Bob: Not if you study a lot! Don't worry, Mary. I'm sure you (5) will / are going to pass it.

/ 5

C Complete the dialogue using the Future Continuous of the verbs in brackets.

Mark: Welcome to our show! Today I (1) _____ (talk) to Barry Tall about his plan to climb Everest. Barry, (2) _____ you _____ (set off) on your journey in the next few days?

Barry: Yes, I'm very excited.

Mark: (3) _____ you _____ (climb) alone or with others?

Barry: With others, Mark. They are eight of us in the group. They (4) _____ (follow) me during the trip.

Mark: Are you worried about getting lost?

Barry: No, I (5) _____ (use) a GPS unit, so I'm sure we'll be OK.

Mark: Sounds like you have an amazing trip ahead of you, Barry!

/ 5

D Write sentences or questions using these words. Use the Future Perfect Simple.

1 Bob / finish / school / June

_____

2 ? / he / take / his exams / tomorrow

_____

3 he / find / a job / at the end of summer

_____

4 ? / Bob / complete / his training / next month

_____

5 he / begin / college / at the age of eighteen

_____

/ 5

Reading

A Read about Jenny and Marco's life plans.

Jenny, 17

I'm interested in having some adventure in my life. I don't want to just finish university and get a job in an office. I'm studying for a degree in journalism and I want to travel around the world and write about what I see. By the time I'm 30, I'll be ready to stop working and have a family. But I'm not going to give up on journalism forever. When my children are old enough for school, I'll use my qualifications as a writer to get a part-time job. Maybe one day I'll write children's books. It's a very nice idea!

Marco, 18

My friends tell me I'm really ambitious and I guess they're right. When I finish university, I want to set up my own camping equipment store. I love camping and enjoying outdoor adventures, so this idea is perfect for me. I plan to sell equipment that people need when they go on expeditions and adventures. Along with things like GPS units and sleeping bags, I'll offer training programmes. My programmes will teach people how to put up a tent, survive in the wild, go rock climbing, and so much more. I'll never give up this dream. I know I can make it work.

Comprehension

B Write R (Right), W (Wrong) or DS (Doesn't say).

1 Jenny is studying how to be a tour guide.

2 Jenny cares about having a family and a career.

3 Marco enjoys the outdoors.

4 Marco is going to university to learn how to start a business.

5 Both people enjoy studying.

/ 10

/ 50

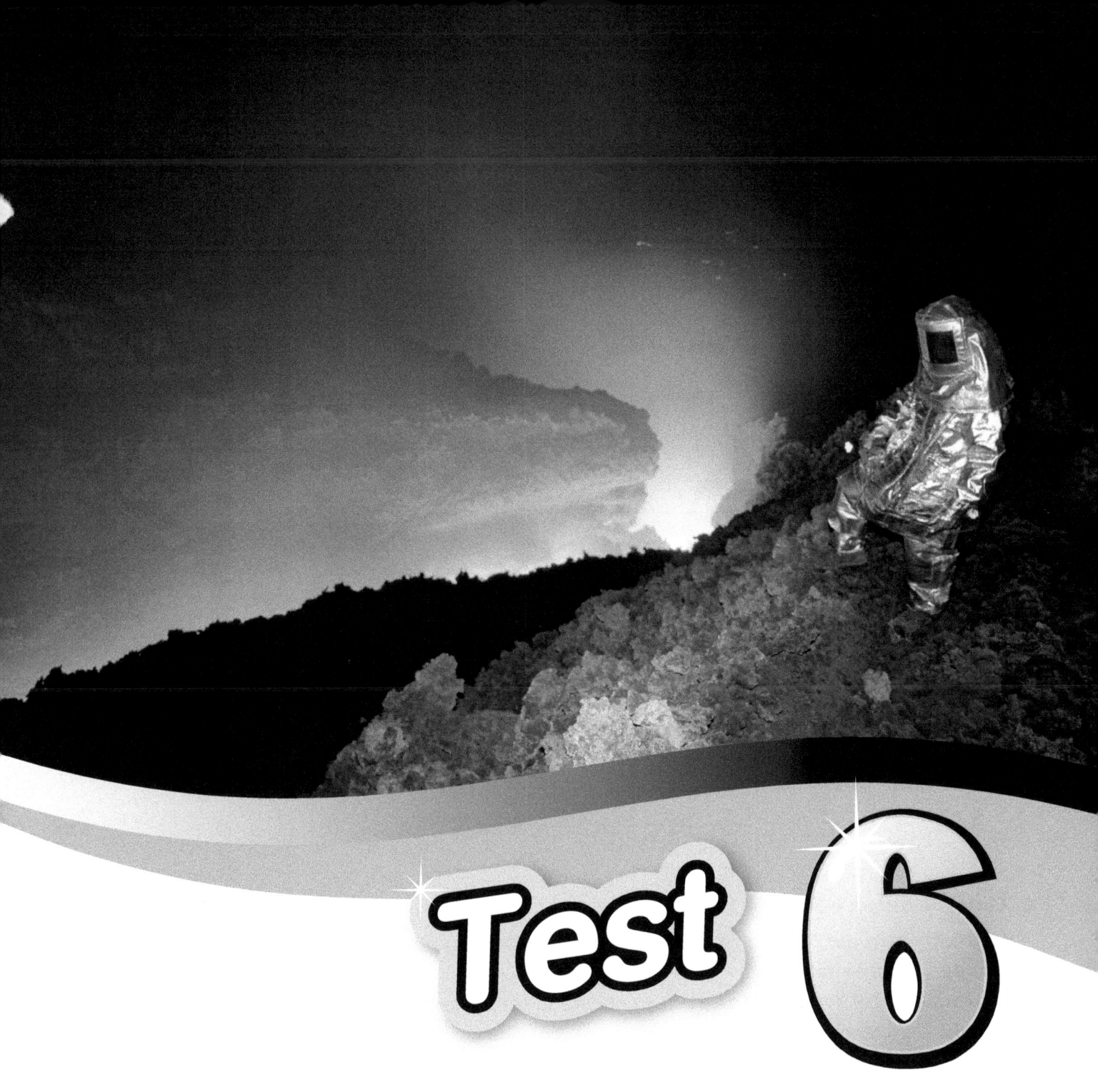

Test 6

6 Remarkable People

Vocabulary

A Complete the sentences with these words.

admire   escape   observe   specimen   voyage

1 Renee travelled to South America to _____ animals for her research.
2 Many people _____ famous actors.
3 Marty collected a plant _____ for scientific research.
4 Christopher Columbus took a long _____ in his ship to travel to America.
5 The woman's family moved away from their country to _____ the war. / 5

B Put the letters in the correct order to find professions.

1 t i r w e r   _____
2 w a y r e l   _____
3 l e e t t a h   _____
4 s c u n m a i i   _____
5 g o t i i l s o b   _____   / 5

C Circle the correct words.

Nathan: Yesterday, I watched a famous photographer (1) take / give some photos of some lions at the zoo.
Mandy: Was it interesting?
Nathan: Sort of. It (2) took / gave him a long time to get the perfect photo.
Mandy: Were there many people there?
Nathan: Not really. The area wasn't very (3) serious / crowded.
Mandy: You know, I like photography. I would like to (4) take / give part in a good photography course in the future.
Nathan: I'm going to the photographer's studio later. I can (5) give / take you a lift and you can ask him if he knows of a good school. / 5

D Match.

1 Janet became a doctor at   a ages, but she looked the same.
2 I hadn't seen her in   b of work for two months now.
3 Mark saw Jeff by   c chance and was quite surprised to see him.
4 Martha is in   d the age of 21.
5 Denise has been out   e her sixties, but she looks about fifty. / 5

Grammar

A Circle the correct words.

(1) To work / Working with plants is a fascinating job. Since I was a child, I have been interested in

(2) to collect / collecting different kinds of plants. Now that I'm a scientist, I have managed

(3) to discover / discovering many new things about plants. This summer I plan (4) to explore / exploring

parts of Brazil, which has many different plant species. I hope (5) to do / doing this work for many more

years to come.

/ 5

B The words in bold are wrong. Write the correct infinitive or gerund.

1 I enjoy **work** on scientific experiments.   _____

2 I sometimes try **helping** my brother with his homework.   _____

3 **Spend** time in a laboratory is enjoyable work.   _____

4 I've decided to **became** a journalist when I go to university. _____

5 We all need **doing** something that we find interesting.   _____   / 5

C Choose the correct answers.

1 Mike was disappointed _____ that the
   woman in the photo had died.
   a   learning
   b   to learn
   c   learn

2 If you want to know about famous people,
   try _____ about them in magazines.
   a   read
   b   reading
   c   to be reading

3 Please stop _____ the sculptures. You will
   damage them.
   a   to touch
   b   touch
   c   touching

4 Lisa is used _____ lots of attention as a
   famous singer.
   a   getting
   b   to getting
   c   get

5 I will never forget _____ my favourite actor
   in that café last year.
   a   seeing
   b   to see
   c   see

6 Margie and John stopped _____ a volcano
   while travelling in Hawaii.
   a   visiting
   b   to visit
   c   visit

7 Will you remember _____ Mary if she's
   coming to the museum tomorrow?
   a   ask
   b   to ask
   c   asking

8 The scientist went on to _____ about his
   remarkable discovery.
   a   talk
   b   talked
   c   talking

9 I remember _____ that man's show on TV
   when I was a child.
   a   to watch
   b   watch
   c   watching

10 Paul was happy _____ skydiving during his
    trip to America.
    a   go
    b   going
    c   to go

/ 10

Reading

A Read about a famous Olympic runner.

Jamaican runner Usain Bolt is a remarkable athlete. At the 2008 Beijing Olympics, he won three races and set a new world record in one of them, the 100-metre race. In addition to the 100-metre race, Bolt also won the 200-metre race and helped his team win the 400-metre race. About 10 metres before the end of the 100-metre race, Bolt realised that he was going to win, so he slowed down and did a little dance! He still managed to win the race, and not only that, he broke the world record as well!

Bolt was born in a small town in Jamaica. When he was young, he was interested in football and cricket. When, his high school teacher saw how fast he ran on the field, however, he told Bolt that he was an excellent runner. Soon after, Bolt began training with the Jamaican national team. In 2001 he won a gold medal and two silver medals at the World Junior Championships in Jamaica. He was only 15 years old, but he was already almost two metres tall.

Bolt first competed in the Olympic Games in 2004. However, he hurt his leg and was not able to run very fast, but that didn't stop him. He continued his training and by 2008 he was winning gold medals at the Beijing Olympics. Today, he is the fastest man in the world!

Comprehension

B Write R (Right), W (Wrong) or DS (Doesn't say).

1 Bolt won the 400-metre race at the 2008 Beijing Olympics by himself.
2 He started dancing after he won the 100-metre race.
3 One of his teachers called him an excellent football player.
4 He was taller than any other athlete on the Jamaican national team.
5 He didn't do well at the 2004 Olympics.

 / 10

Total / 50

Mid-Year Test

Mid-Year Test

Vocabulary

A Match.

1 telescope ☐
2 axe ☐
3 shovel ☐
4 rocket ☐
5 sculpture ☐

/ 5

B Complete the word groups.

| career | pleasant | scales | tsunami | writer |

1 flood   earthquake   _____
2 wing   horn   _____
3 lawyer   politician   _____
4 careful   patient   _____
5 occupation   profession   _____

/ 5

C Write the missing letters.

1 This happens after a long time with no rain.   d _ _ _ _ _ _ _
2 This describes someone who is often happy.   c _ _ _ _ _ _ _ _
3 You can look closely at the stars in this place.   o _ _ _ _ _ _ _ _ _ _ _
4 Kings and queens live in these.   p _ _ _ _ _ _ _
5 This happens when two countries fight.   w _ _

/ 5

D Choose the correct answers.

1 The teacher told Mark not to _____ on becoming an astronaut.
  a turn up
  b turn down
  c give up

2 Lisa, will you please _____ the car? We're going to be late!
  a check in
  b get in
  c get on

3 Paul's uncle was a biologist _____, but now he doesn't work any more.
  a in comparison
  b on purpose
  c for ages

4 Did you _____ finding the answer to your question?
  a search for
  b succeed in
  c depend on

5 Is this coat _____ cold weather?
  a suitable for
  b responsible for
  c capable of

/ 5

E Complete the sentences with these words.

| athlete | criminal | employer | journalist | volunteer |

1 The police found the _____ hiding in an old building.
2 The _____ wrote an impressive article on the famous woman.
3 My dad's _____ is called Mr Jones.
4 Thomas started working as a(n) _____, but now he gets paid.
5 The _____ came first in the running competition.

/ 5

F Circle the correct words.

1 Maria doesn't like to spend money. She's very stingy / dishonest.
2 David made / did a mistake on his homework and lost a mark.
3 I read a leaflet / specimen about recycling this morning.
4 After not eating for two days, Amos felt very brave / weak.
5 This book gave / took me some good ideas for choosing a career.

/ 5

Grammar

A Circle the correct words.

Sarah: Hi Mike. How was your summer?

Mike: You'll never believe it, Sarah. There was a big hurricane (1) when / which I was in Florida.

Sarah: Really? How scary!

Mike: Yes, it was. I don't know (2) who / what was more afraid, me or my father. My aunt, (3) which / whose house we were staying in, wasn't afraid at all.

Sarah: Did you know it was coming?

Mike: No, we didn't. The hurricane, (4) which / when was called Hurricane Fred, was a complete surprise. We had no idea (5) where / which it came from!

/ 5

B Choose the correct answers.

1 Mirta _____ for the perfect job every day for several months.
  a looks   b has looked   c has been looking

2 Ali thinks that he _____ a new job, but he's not sure.
  a has found   b was finding   c had been finding

3 Kevin didn't want to go on holiday in Spain because he _____ there already.
  a had travelled   b travelled   c will travel

4 I'm sure she will _____ the project by the end of the year.
  a be finishing   b have finished   c have been finishing

5 Renee _____ a new dress in a department store last week.
  a buys   b bought   c has bought

/ 5

C Complete the conversation with the verbs in brackets using the Future Simple or be going to.

Tina: Martin, have you thought about your career?

Martin: Definitely. I (1) _____ (be) a journalist after I finish college.

Tina: That's a good profession. I think you (2) _____ (do) well as one.

Martin: Thanks, Tina. What about you? (3) _____ you _____ (start) college soon?

Tina: Yes, I am. I'm quite excited about it. I (4) _____ (study) art and
             music because I love them both. I don't know what career to follow yet, but I can decide later.

Martin: You can always ask me for advice. I (5) _____ (help) you find a career!

/ 5

D Complete the sentences with gerunds or infinitives made from the verbs in brackets.

1 Remarkable people manage _____ (do) things the rest of us can't.

2 John isn't afraid of _____ (try) new and unusual things.

3 My grandparents are interested in _____ (learn) as much as they can.

4 Michelle went on _____ (study) even after she finished college.

5 Did John decide _____ (spend) the whole day in the library?

/ 5

E Complete the sentences with the comparative or superlative of these words.

badly   difficult   fast   little   near

1 Everyone would agree that cars travel _____ bicycles.

2 I think maths is _____ school subject.

3 Mary shops at that market because it's _____ one to her house.

4 Out of all her friends, Jill works _____ . She only works part-time.

5 Janet did _____ on her history test than her science test.

/ 5

F Circle the correct words.

The legend of Odysseus is famous all over the world. Odysseus was a Greek king who (1) has lived / lived on the
island of Ithaca in ancient times. The legend says that Odysseus left Ithaca to fight in the Trojan War, and after
he and his men had helped win the war, they (2) were beginning / began the journey back to Ithaca. While
Odysseus (3) was returning / returned home, he faced many difficult situations and almost didn't make it back.
When he (4) arrived / had arrived on the island twenty years after he had left, many people on the island didn't
know who he was. They (5) didn't see / hadn't seen him for so long!

/ 5

Reading

A Read this article about unusual species of fish.

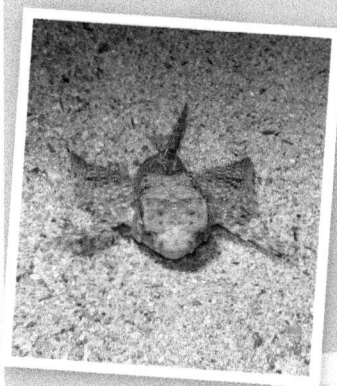

The flying gurnard

The flying gurnard lives in the ocean waters around eastern North America. Its name sounds like the name of a bird, and you can understand why by looking at it. The flying gurnard is easy to recognise because it seems to have big wings on its back. These are actually very large fins, or flat parts of a fish's body that help it swim. The flying gurnard uses its fins to swim along slowly in shallow water looking for food. Because of its 'wings', people used to believe that it could fly.

The stonefish

The stonefish lives in the Pacific and Indian Oceans. If you take one look at this fish, you can see how it got its name. It looks like a big rock sitting on the bottom of the ocean. The stonefish may be one of the ugliest fish in the world, but being ugly isn't always bad. Because it looks like a rock, most of its enemies don't notice it. It just sits quietly on the ocean floor and eats small fish that swim by. Using this method, the stonefish gets all the food it needs!

The seahorse

The seahorse is probably one of the strangest underwater animals you will ever see. Its head actually looks very much like a small horse's head. There are about 35 different species of seahorse. They live in warm waters in oceans all over the world. There is something quite unusual about this species. The father, instead of the mother, takes care of the baby seahorses until they are capable of swimming and taking care of themselves. This lasts from 10 days to six weeks. Another interesting fact is that a father and mother seahorse remain with each other for a very long time – sometimes up to five years!

Comprehension

B Write F (flying gurnard), ST (stonefish) or SH (seahorse).
Which animal...

1 doesn't move around a lot?
2 hunts for food in shallow water?
3 lives in more than one ocean?
4 has parents that stay together?

/ 10

Writing

Write an article giving your opinion about public transport. Use this plan to help you.

Paragraph 1
Introduce topic by talking about the variety of public transport available and the need to use it to cut down on pollution.

Paragraph 2
Talk about public transport in your country, what there is, who uses it, if it's expensive, reliable, etc.

Paragraph 3
Suggest ways of encouraging more people to use public transport.

Paragraph 4
Give your opinion about public transport - say why we should use it, etc.

/ 10

Total / 80

Test 7

7 Mind and Body

Vocabulary

A Circle the correct words.

1 My parents are going on holiday this weekend for some experiment / relaxation.
2 These days many women in magazines look too skinny / tiny.
3 I'll take up yoga if you are fascinating / willing to do it with me.
4 Lesley has been very stressed / scary lately with all the work she has to do.
5 My grandfather is exhausted / terrified of hospitals, so I usually go with him.

/ 5

B Write the missing letters.

1 This is a place where you can buy pills. c _ _ _ _ _ _
2 This is two or more things mixed together. c _ _ _ _ _ _ _ _ _ _
3 Your throat can feel this way. s _ _ _ _
4 This is usually a very beautiful person. m _ _ _ _ _
5 This describes something really big. e _ _ _ _ _ _ _ _

/ 5

C Complete the sentences with these words.

catch   join   keep   lose   take

1 People usually _____ colds in winter.
2 I plan to _____ a gym in the new year.
3 Did you _____ much weight on your diet?
4 Does he often _____ pills for his headaches?
5 Vicky tries to _____ fit by exercising daily.

/ 5

D Choose the correct answers.

1 The company is going to bring _____ some new beauty products this autumn.
   a on   b out   c in
2 You should try _____ clothes to see if they fit before you buy them.
   a on   b for   c out
3 Take _____ your shoes and make yourself comfortable.
   a out   b off   c up
4 These hats are too silly to wear. I don't think they will catch _____ .
   a up with   b up   c on
5 Has Margie finished putting _____ her make-up yet?
   a on   b off   c down

/ 5

Grammar

A Complete the sentences using these words or phrases.

> can   can't   could   couldn't   was able

1 I was a great runner when I was twelve. I _____ run six kilometres!
2 Emma, _____ you call in at the chemist later today?
3 Even though Mark had a bad headache last night, he _____ to go to sleep.
4 Thomas is only 5 years old. He _____ go to the gym until he's older.
5 The woman didn't make it to hospital in time, so the doctors _____ save her.   ◯ / 5

B Circle the correct words.

Mary: Julie has been taking yoga classes for years now. She (1) may / must really like it.

Susan: I know. I (2) might / must start taking classes too, but I haven't decided yet.

Mary: Let's both start!

Susan: Well, I (3) may be / maybe taking an extra class at school. I don't want to get stressed by having too many things to do.

Mary: True, but the yoga class (4) might / must keep you from becoming stressed.

Susan: Yes, but I'm sure it (5) might not / can't be good to take too many classes!   ◯ / 5

C Choose the correct answers.

1 Our dog is enormous. She _____ lose weight.
   a have to   b will have   c has to
2 Don't forget your books! You _____ leave them at the house again.
   a must   b don't have to   c mustn't
3 _____ take this yoga class together?
   a Ought we   b Should we   c We ought to
4 You _____ exercise every day of the week. It isn't necessary.
   a don't have to   b mustn't   c won't have to
5 Michael _____ to stop watching so much TV.
   a must   b should   c ought   ◯ / 5

D Put the words in the correct order to make sentences or questions.

1 able / was / go / to / yesterday / I / not / swimming

_____

2 this / join / David / might / gym / a / year

_____

3 after / ate / exercise / Jill / dinner / couldn't / she

_____

4 ? / have / go / to / Ali / to / hospital / did

_____

5 running / must / ten / tired / they / be / after / kilometres

_____

◯ / 5

Reading

A Read about Kim and her experiences doing yoga.

A few months ago I started going to a gym. My main purpose was to exercise more and become fitter. My doctor also told me I should probably lose some weight. I enjoyed my time at the gym and I started to lose weight and have more energy. Then one day after about six weeks I saw a sign that read 'Free Beginner Yoga Class—5:00 every Tuesday'. I decided to go to a class or two to see if I'd like it.

On the first day I didn't know what to expect, but the teacher, Devi Rose, was amazing! She was so cheerful and patient. First of all, she showed us new breathing exercises. We practised concentrating on our breathing, taking very deep breaths and letting the air out slowly. Then Devi showed us how to do several different exercises. At first I couldn't do some of them. My body just wouldn't move the right way, but I never gave up. Ater a few weeks, I was able to do most of them.

At the end of each class my body was exhausted, but at the same time my mind felt very calm. I noticed that I could concentrate on my work better after doing yoga. I also began to sleep better. In the past I had difficulty sleeping, but after two months of yoga I didn't have any problems falling asleep at all! I'm not sure how yoga works, but it does. I have even succeeded in getting a couple of my friends to come to class with me!

Comprehension

B Answer the questions.

1 What advice did Kim get before joining a gym?

_____

2 Why did Kim take up yoga?

_____

3 What was the first thing Kim learned in her yoga class?

_____

4 What was Kim not able to do at the beginning of the class?

_____

5 What problem did Kim have at bedtime?

_____

/ 10

 Total / 50

Test 8

Vocabulary

A Write the missing letters.

1 This is something we use to make music.   i _ _ _ _ _ _ _ _ _ _

2 This is the difference between two things.   c _ _ _ _ _ _ _ _

3 This describes something kind and calm.   g _ _ _ _ _ _

4 Plays and books are this.   l _ _ _ _ _ _ _ _ _

5 This is a large group of people.   c _ _ _ _ _   / 5

B Choose the correct answers.

1 There was a mountain in the _____ of the painting.
  a atmosphere   b close-up   c background

2 What are they saying in this song? I can't understand the _____ .
  a rhythms   b roots   c lyrics

3 Sarah painted a lovely _____ of the two children.
  a portrait   b landscape   c frame

4 She doesn't look nice in the picture because she was in a bad _____ .
  a mood   b style   c flow

5 Robert, would you like to _____ your photos with the class?
  a share   b remind   c express   / 5

C Complete the sentences with these words.

classical	composer	graffiti	loud	scene

1 Her neighbour's music was so _____ that Mary couldn't sleep.

2 A lot of _____ music was written in the 1700s.

3 Many buildings in the centre have _____ all over the outside walls.

4 The _____ worked for hours creating his music.

5 My favourite _____ of the play was at the very end.   / 5

D Circle the correct words.

1 Pedro is an expert on / of classical music.

2 What is your attitude for / to rap music?

3 There is a need of / for more good composers in Hollywood.

4 She isn't a lover on / of modern art.

5 Music has a good effect on / of most children.   / 5

Grammar

A The words in bold are wrong. Write the correct words.

1 A new movie is **be** shown in the library right now. _____

2 Music CDs can be **took** from the library overnight. _____

3 The musician was **gived** a reward for his work. _____

4 The concert was **enjoy** by over 100 people. _____

5 The songs were **write** by a famous composer. _____

 / 5

B Circle the correct words.

Sam: That's a very beautiful picture.

Tina: I agree. It (1) was painted / painted over 100 years ago. Did you know it (2) is / was once stolen from this museum?

Sam: Really?

Tina: Yes. Actually, it (3) has been / was being taken twice. Last year, it was (4) sent / being sent to another museum when someone took it from the lorry.

Sam: No way!

Tina: I know. I can't imagine it will be (5) stolen / stealing again.

 / 5

C Complete the second sentences so that they have the same meaning as the first sentences. Use the passive voice.

1 The teacher showed the movie to the class.

The movie _____ .

2 Famous journalists interview famous musicians.

Famous musicians _____ .

3 Do hip hop artists perform rap music at concerts?

_____ rap music _____ ?

4 Her parents didn't send her to a music school.

She _____ .

5 Children don't study classical music.

Classical music _____ . / 5

D Complete the poster with the correct passive form of the verbs in brackets.

This weekend, Laurel High School is putting on the yearly student art exhibition in Gilbert Hall. Everyone (1) _____ (encourage) to come! Art work (2) _____ (can / see) from 10 am to 6 pm on Saturday and Sunday. Food and drinks (3) _____ (serve) and music (4) _____ (perform) by local bands. This is one show that (5) _____ (should / not miss)!

/ 5

Reading

A Read about this famous museum.

The Guggenheim Museum in New York City doesn't look like a traditional art museum. The museum was built in an unusual style in which the walls were made to look like circles that become larger the higher they go. Because the building is so different from other buildings around it, it seems that the museum itself is a work of art.

The history of the museum goes back to the late 1920s. Solomon R. Guggenheim, a wealthy American, began collecting art with the help of his friend, Hilla Rebay, a German painter. At first, the artwork was shown in Guggenheim's New York City home. The exhibition was of contemporary paintings by famous modern artists. Then, in 1939, Guggenheim and Rebay opened a museum on East 54th Street in New York City in a building where cars were once sold. However, the space soon became too small to hold all the art.

In 1943, Guggenheim decided that he was going to build the most unusual modern museum that the world had even seen. The building of the Guggenheim Museum started that year at a site on 89th Street near New York City's Central Park. The museum took fifteen years to complete. It was finally opened in the autumn of 1959. Most people loved it for its unusual appearance, but some people didn't. They thought the building's appearance made the art inside the building seem less impressive. It was certainly different from anything people had ever seen before.

The Guggenheim is now a world famous museum. It has been shown in movies like *Men in Black*, *The International* and *Bye Bye Birdie*. In 2009, fifty years after its opening, much of the museum was painted and made to look new. Today, it looks as good as it did when it was first built.

THE SOLOMON R GUGGENHEIM MUSEUM

Comprehension

B Choose the correct answers.

1 The Guggenheim Museum is like a work of art because it _____
   a was built by an artist.
   b isn't the same as other buildings.
   c is in New York City.

2 Solomon R. Guggenheim's home was used _____
   a to show art.
   b to make paintings.
   c as a home for artists.

3 Guggenheim's first museum building _____
   a was also a work of art.
   b once had cars in it.
   c was also his home.

4 The Guggenheim Museum can now be found _____
   a at Guggenheim's apartment.
   b on 54th Street.
   c near Central Park.

5 The museum was painted _____
   a fifty years ago.
   b only when it was first built.
   c in 2009.

/ 10

Total / 50

Test 9

Extreme Sports

Vocabulary

A Match.

1 You put a wetsuit   a on your feet.
2 Flippers go   b on your hands.
3 You wear goggles   c over your eyes.
4 Gloves go   d over your chest.
5 You place a life jacket   e over your whole body.

/ 5

B Circle the correct words.

1 Hannah believes she can aim / beat all her competitors.
2 Mark hit / scored the winning goal in the last minute of the game.
3 Jackie learned how to surf / ride in the ocean when she was eight.
4 How long was it before the skydivers landed / came after they jumped?
5 Be careful not to lean / slip too far over the edge.

/ 5

C Write the missing letters.

1 This is a formal celebration.   c _ _ _ _ _ _ _
2 This is like a wall of water in the ocean.   w _ _ _
3 This is something that is not easy to do.   c _ _ _ _ _ _ _ _
4 This is something you wear when you jump out of a plane.   p _ _ _ _ _ _ _
5 This is worn over your chest when you climb rocks.   h _ _ _ _ _ _

/ 5

D Complete the sentences with these phrases.

catch up with	drop out of	get the hang of	warm up	work out

1 Mike took ten minutes to _____ before he started his exercises.
2 Lee told his friend not to _____ the competition.
3 They usually _____ for two hours every day at the gym.
4 Erin couldn't _____ the lead cyclist so she lost the race.
5 Michael stopped paragliding because he couldn't _____ it.

/ 5

Grammar

A The words in bold are wrong. Write the correct words.

1 If you exercise a lot, you will **became** strong.   _____

2 If the waves **will be** big, she'll go surfing.   _____

3 They will **had** a party if they win the game.   _____

4 You must wear a wetsuit if you **went** into the ocean.   _____

5 I **wore** goggles if I go swimming this afternoon.   _____   / 5

B Circle the correct words.

1 It's OK to go in the water unless / if it looks dangerous.

2 If you try / don't try bungee jumping, you won't know how much fun it is.

3 If / Unless you want to ride in the boat, you must wear a lifejacket.

4 You should / shouldn't borrow my wetsuit unless you've already got one.

5 I will go surfing on Friday unless / if I'm not too busy.   / 5

C Choose the correct answers.

1 If it _____ so scary, Mary would
go skydiving.
  a were
  b was
  c weren't

2 If he didn't have to work so much,
he _____ the marathon.
  a wouldn't run
  b would run
  c is running

3 If I were you, I _____ stand at the edge of that cliff.
  a couldn't
  b won't
  c wouldn't

4 If someone offered to take you on holiday,
where _____ want to go?
  a will you
  b would you
  c you would

5 They would go for a ride on their mountain
bikes if it _____ .
  a would rain
  b weren't raining
  c wouldn't rain

/ 5

D Complete the dialogue with the correct form of the verbs in brackets.

Jason: Hilary, did you hear about Martin's accident?

Hilary: Yes, I did. I'm not surprised. If he had had his harness on,
he (1) _____ (not fall) from that rock.

Jason: In addition to that, he wouldn't have hurt his head if he
(2) _____ (buy) a better helmet like I told him to.

Hilary: It wasn't the best weather either. If it hadn't rained that
morning, the rocks (3) _____ (not be) wet.

Jason: Exactly! And would he (4) _____ (slip)
if he had worn better shoes for the trip?

Hilary: I don't know, but the good news is that he's doing OK.
If his friends (5) _____ (not take)
him to hospital in a hurry, he would have been
in serious trouble!

/ 5

Reading

A Read about these three friends and the sports they love.

Michael, 19

If it's summer and I have the time to drive two hours to the sea, I go scuba diving. It's my favourite free-time activity during warm months. My father's best friend was a scuba diving instructor, and I first went to scuba diving school when I was 10 years old. In the beginning I could only go in water that was 10 feet deep, but now I dive in water that's 40 or 50 feet deep. It's important to go down into the water very slowly as well as come up slowly. If you don't do this, it can be very painful. I still get afraid if a big fish starts to follow me, but it usually goes away after a few minutes. If I decide to become a scuba diving teacher after college, I will open my own scuba diving school!

Anna, 15

My favourite sport is windsurfing, although it's a hard sport to learn. You must have a strong body to do it. If you have strength in your arms and legs, the sport becomes much easier. When I took my first windsurfing lessons a few weeks ago, I spent a day or two just learning how to stand up on the board. Later on, I took the board onto a large lake behind my house. I fell off a lot at first, but it didn't bother me. Now I sail around the middle of the lake for hours. I've learnt to use the power of the wind to go really fast. Sometimes I still fall in the water, but I just get up and start all over again.

Joanna, 16

I've loved skiing ever since I was a child. I can remember when my family and I used to visit my uncle, who is a ski instructor, at his house in the mountains. My uncle loved to ski. If the mountains were covered in fresh snow, he would go skiing. He taught me how to ski when I was just 6 years old. We started off going down very small hills, then we tried bigger hills. That was scary for me. I was afraid I might fall over the edge of a cliff! I've practised a lot since then, but I'm still not as comfortable with the sport as I'd like to be. If it was possible, I would practise every single day!

Comprehension

B Write M (Michael), A (Anna) or J (Joanna).
   Who...

1 learnt his/her sport from a relative? ☐

2 would like to practise all the time ☐

3 would like to teach others how to do his/her sport? ☐

4 does his/her sport close to home? ☐

5 learnt his/her sport recently? ☐

/ 10

Total / 50

Test 10

10 Crime

Vocabulary

A Write P (person), O (object) or C (crime).

1 robbery ☐
2 judge ☐
3 handcuffs ☐
4 murder ☐
5 burglar ☐

6 axe ☐
7 prisoner ☐
8 robber ☐
9 victim ☐
10 arrow ☐

◯ / 10

B Circle the correct words.

1 The police called / arrested the criminal as he was running from the crime scene.
2 Three people stole / robbed a bank last night.
3 It's the job of the courts to punish criminals when they commit / break crimes.
4 One thing laws are supposed to do is protect innocent / fair people.
5 Thomas lost his bag because he was being very careless / embarrassing with it.

◯ / 5

C Complete the sentences with these words.

about   for   into   of   with

1 Jill had an argument _____ Denise for over an hour.
2 Can you explain the reason _____ his bad attitude?
3 That's the man I saw stealing the money. There's no doubt _____ it.
4 The police still haven't discovered the cause _____ the fire.
5 There was an investigation _____ the accident to see if it was a crime.

◯ / 5

Grammar

A Circle the correct words.

Sam: My brother was arrested for driving too fast again yesterday.

Rita: That's terrible! I wish he (1) isn't / **wasn't** such a fast driver.

Sam: It's funny you should say that. He wishes he (2) **were** / had been a racing driver. I think he will be one day!

Rita: Well, I wish I (3) were / **had been** with him before he was arrested. I would have asked him to slow down.

Sam: Yes, if only he (4) listened / **would listen**.

Rita: Exactly! I wish he (5) understands / **understood** how dangerous it is to drive so fast!

 / 5

B Choose the correct answers.

1 They wish they _____ about the accident before they moved into the house.
   a know
   b knew
   c had known

2 He wishes that his friend _____ not guilty.
   a is
   b was
   c would be

3 The crime scene was terrible. She wishes she _____ it.
   a hadn't seen
   b didn't see
   c doesn't see

4 If only we _____ any criminals in the world.
   a don't have
   b didn't have
   c haven't had

5 If only she _____ stealing. She's been arrested twice.
   a can stop
   b could stop
   c stops

 / 5

C Circle the correct words.

1 The criminal cut himself / herself when he broke through the window.

2 Don't worry too much on holiday. Enjoy ourselves / yourself.

3 She didn't want Joseph to go with her. She went to the police with / by herself.

4 Don't blame yourself / her for the accident. She didn't mean to do it.

5 Did someone help him solve the murder, or did he solve it himself / itself?

6 They told themselves / ourselves not to be afraid.

7 The animal hurt itself / himself when it tried to escape.

8 Paul was going to steal a CD, but his friend told him / himself not to do it.

9 The leaflets are free, so please help yourselves / themselves.

10 I wouldn't talk to / by yourself if I were you. People may think you're strange.

 / 10

Reading

A Read this report on crime.

SMALL CRIMES ARE STILL CRIMES!

Smaller crimes aren't as serious as murder or robbery, but they can create a situation in which more serious crimes can happen. These crimes often don't have just one victim – they affect everyone. Here are some examples:

Littering

Although littering doesn't seem like it hurts anyone, it makes a neighbourhood look dirty. If a neighbourhood is full of litter and has a bad appearance, it may seem like there aren't any police in the area. Criminals then think they can commit serious crimes and they won't be punished. So, if people are punished more often for littering, neighbourhoods will look cleaner and dangerous criminals may stay away.

Graffiti

Some people say graffiti is art, but if you are the owner of a building or home with graffiti on it, you might not feel the same way. In most countries, if you paint something on the side of a building without getting permission, you are breaking the law. While some graffiti is attractive, most of it makes buildings and neighbourhoods look ugly. For people who like their neighbourhoods nice and clean, it isn't fair that they have to look at graffiti.

Noise

Many countries have laws about noise. These laws exist to punish people for making lots of noise, such as playing loud music in their homes, on the street or on a bus. It's a fact that noise can cause problems with people's health. It can also cause arguments to break out between neighbours. Of course, the arguments make more noise! So think twice before you play your music as loud as you can.

Comprehension

B Answer the questions.

1 Who is affected by smaller crimes like littering, graffiti and noise?

_____

2 What can happen in a neighbourhood that is full of litter?

_____

3 Who might not think graffiti is art?

_____

4 Why do noise laws exist?

_____

5 What does loud noise cause?

_____

/ 10

Total  / 50

Test 11

11 Communication

Vocabulary

A Circle the correct words.

Anna: Do you like your new computer, Mike?

Mike: Yes, I do. The only (1) drawback / connection is that it's very slow when I'm on the Internet.

Anna: Oh really? So how long does it take you to (2) download / visit a file?

Mike: It takes ages!

Anna: Maybe there's a problem with your (3) card / modem. I imagine the shop can fix it. Apart from that, are you happy with the computer?

Mike: Yes, it's great, actually. I bought this computer because it has a nice (4) audio / marine system.

Anna: Well, hopefully the shop can fix the problem without making you pay any extra (5) surveys / charges!

/ 5

B Complete the sentences with these words.

> delete   enter   log on   play   surf

1 Did you _____ your information into the web site correctly?
2 I think there's a problem with your computer. I can't _____ any DVDs on it.
3 You have to _____ to the website before you can look at your personal information.
4 If you _____ the Internet for too many hours, your eyes will become very tired!
5 Don't _____ this message. It contains some very important information.

/ 5

C Choose the correct answers.

1 Mary _____ a speech on communication in today's world.
   a told   b made   c spoke
2 This message was written using numbers. Can you _____ it so we can read it?
   a decode   b whistle   c identify
3 The woman didn't answer her phone, so Frank _____ a message.
   a had   b made   c left
4 Paul is a very busy man. He has to _____ at least 50 emails every day.
   a write   b enter   c pay for
5 Nancy _____ online and booked a hotel for her holiday.
   a made   b had   c went

/ 5

D Match.

1 They used to be friends, but they don't get   a off for using his computer too much.
2 Frank made   b across to everyone in the class.
3 Martin was able to get his ideas   c up a silly story about how he could understand dolphins.
4 He told his brother   d through.
5 Harry tried calling his sister, but he couldn't get   e on very well anymore.

/ 5

Grammar

A The words in bold are wrong. Write the correct words.

Good communication is not always easy in my house. Last night Mum was sending an email when
Dad arrived home. He asked her what we **are** (1) _____ having for dinner and
she said 'pasta'. Dad said he didn't **wanted** (2) _____ pasta again because we had
had it the **following** (3) _____ day as well. Mum **said** (4) _____
him that she hadn't **have** (5) _____ time to make anything else and that she was busy at
the (6) _____ moment. She told Dad to **cooking** (7) _____ something
himself if he wanted something different and Dad asked **if** (8) _____ he should cook.
Mum told him she **doesn't** (9) _____ have time to think about it
now (10) _____ . Then Dad went to the phone and ordered a pizza!

/ 10

B Write the sentences using direct speech.

1 Bill said he had found his watch.   _____

2 Judy asked where that phone was from.   _____

3 Patrick asked if Carrie had bought a computer.   _____

4 Mrs Peters told the children to put their books away.   _____

5 The man asked Kyle to close the window.   _____

/ 5

C Complete the sentences using reported speech.

1 'Is Ben going to the park tomorrow?' he asked.
   He asked _____ .

2 'The scientist's big speech is tonight,' John said.
   John said _____ .

3 'Where is Jane at the moment?' Mum asked.
   Mum asked _____ .

4 'Why aren't your new clothes here?' Martin asked his son.
   Martin asked his son _____ .

5 'I gave Mr Brant the report a week ago,' Mary told Lisa.
   Mary told Lisa _____ .

/ 5

Reading

A Read about a form of communication.

There are many different ways in which we communicate. Most people would say that words are the main form of communication. In the 1960s, however, communication researcher Albert Mehrabian said most of our communication happened without a single sound coming from our mouths! This form of communication is called body language, which is when we communicate with our faces and bodies.

There are many ways in which we communicate with our bodies. One form of body language is when we cross our arms in front of us. This can mean a number of things. For example, if you're at a party and you're standing with your arms crossed, it can show that you don't want anyone to talk to you. If you are in the middle of a serious conversation and you suddenly do this, it can mean that you don't agree with the other person's ideas. In a friendly conversation, however, it can mean that you are simply thinking about what the other person is saying. Of course, sometimes people cross their arms just because they feel cold!

Another form of body language is eye contact. Most people have been taught from an early age that it is good to have eye contact with people when you speak to them. It shows that you are interested in what they are saying. It is especially important to make eye contact with someone you don't know when you are trying to make a good impression. Be careful, though. Even though eye contact is necessary to make a good impression, other forms of body langauge can cause the opposite to happen if used at the same time. If you're making eye contact with someone who's talking to you and also using your hands to play with a pen or some papers, then it shows you're just acting like you're interested. The truth is, you're really bored!

Comprehension

B Choose the correct answers.

1 Albert Mehrabian said that we communicate mostly with our _____
   a words.
   b mouths.
   c bodies.

2 One way we communicate with our bodies is we _____
   a stand in one place.
   b cross our arms.
   c sit at a party.

3 In a serious conversation, crossing your arms means you _____ what's being said.
   a don't agree with
   b don't want to talk about
   c aren't thinking about

4 Making eye contact with people shows that you are _____
   a interested.
   b important.
   c careful.

5 People will think you're _____ if you look at them and play with pens while they're talking.
   a interested in them
   b making a good impression
   c really bored

/ 10

Total / 50

Test 12

Vocabulary

A Write the missing letters.

1 This is another word for money.   c _ _ _ _
2 Something gives you this if it makes you happy.   p _ _ _ _ _ _ _ _
3 This describes the kind of clothing you wear for important events.   f _ _ _ _ _ _
4 This is a type of small clothing store.   b _ _ _ _ _ _ _ _
5 You get this piece of paper when you buy something.   r _ _ _ _ _ _   / 5

B Complete the sentences with these words.

> bargain   comfort   experiment   high-tech   version

1 That shirt is a(n) _____ at only five euros.
2 Maybe another shop has a cheaper _____ of this shoe.
3 My mum is more interested in _____ than style. She would rather feel good than look good.
4 This pen is quite _____ . You can save computer files on it!
5 Renee is doing a(n) _____ to see if she can avoid buying any clothes for a year!   / 5

C Circle the correct words.

1 The queue / price was too long so I didn't buy the dress.
2 Those shoes are too tight / baggy for me.
3 The store deserved / delivered the box to my house.
4 He spends a fortune / cost on stylish clothes.
5 Alice bought three new tips / outfits yesterday.   / 5

D Choose the correct answers.

1 Those shoes cost _____ a hundred euros.
   a at
   b over
   c on

2 The jeans are _____ special offer this week.
   a at
   b over
   c on

3 The shop on Centre Street has many great books _____ sale.
   a for
   b by
   c to

4 They don't have those slippers _____ my size.
   a for
   b in
   c at

5 Black dresses never go out _____ fashion.
   a of
   b in
   c for   / 5

Grammar

A The words in bold are wrong. Write the correct words.

1 She is having a white dress **make** for her wedding.   _____

2 Mark had his shoes **to fix** last week.   _____

3 Is she having her hair **doing** when she goes shopping?   _____

4 Did you have the new television **deliver** to your house ?   _____

5 Is he having his suit **cleaning** at the shop next door?   _____   / 5

B Choose the correct answers.

1 We couldn't carry home all the boxes, so we had _____
   a delivered two boxes.   b two boxes delivered.   c to deliver two boxes.

2 The two girls _____ at a photo shop while they were out shopping.
   a had taken their photo   b took their photo   c had their photo taken

3 My coat was dirty, so _____
   a I had cleaned.   b I had it cleaning.   c I had it cleaned.

4 Her shoe is broken, so she's having _____
   a fixed it.   b it fixed.   c to fix.

5 Mary was going to a party, so she _____
   a has her hair done.   b will have done her hair.   c had her hair done.   / 5

C Circle the correct words.

Tony and Rita went shopping yesterday (1) in order to / in spite of the bad weather. They left the house early (2) despite / so that they could get to the shopping centre before the crowds. (3) Although / Despite they had hurried, the shopping centre was already full of people! (4) In spite of / So that the terrible crowds, Tony and Rita decided to stay and shop.

(5) In order to / So that complete their shopping faster, Tony and Rita decided not to do their shopping together. Tony was looking for winter clothes and shoes (6) so that / in spite of he could have something warm to wear. Rita, however, wanted to buy something nice to wear for her new job (7) in order to / in spite of make a good impression with her boss.

While Tony was shopping, he noticed many bargains still available (8) despite / although the fact that the shopping centre was very crowded. He bought two pairs of shoes and a stylish winter coat. Rita, unfortunately, couldn't find anything she liked. (9) Although / In spite of there were lots a bargains, Rita went home without buying anything.

On the way home, Rita spotted an interesting dress in a second-hand shop. Luckily, it was the perfect size, and (10) despite / although the fact that it was a bit old-fashioned, Rita was quite happy with it!   / 10

Reading

A Read this email about a trip to a market in London.

Email

New   Reply   Forward   Print   Delete

Hi Carrie,

How's it going? Hope you're well. (1) _____
I wanted to tell you about the amazing day
I had with my family at Camden Market.

First of all, I've never seen so many interesting
and colourful shops in my life! All the shops
are small, as there are no department stores,
and some have very unusual appearances.
(2) _____ This one shop that sells leather items
has a huge model aeroplane hanging upside
down over the front door. It's so cool!

Another great thing about the market is the variety of products available. There's no need to go
anywhere else to find what you need. The shops sell everything ranging from designer clothes to
second-hand items, and there are antique shops with great bargains. There are shops that sell CDs
and DVDs, and some sell furniture and televisions. (3) _____ We saw a couple having tattoos put on
their arms, but I wasn't too keen on that. The best thing on offer of course is the clothes. I picked
up a very fashionable pair of blue jeans and my mum bought some high heels. My dad and brother
each got a pair of boots and my brother also got some CDs and a book on pets.

The last thing I'll tell you about before I let you go is the food. A lot of places sell fast food, but there
were a few interesting restaurants serving Indian, Spanish and Brazilian food. (4) _____

Well, that's all for now. (5) _____ Talk to you when I return!

Take care,

Betsy

Comprehension

B Complete the email with these sentences.

a We decided to go for Spanish, and I loved it!

b There are some unusual sights as well.

c I hope you're getting on OK with your studies.

d I'm sending you an email from an Internet café in London.

e The buildings they're in are painted blue, green, red and yellow and have amazing things
   hanging outside on the walls.

 / 10

 / 50

End-of-Year Test

End-of-Year Test

Vocabulary

A Circle the odd one out.

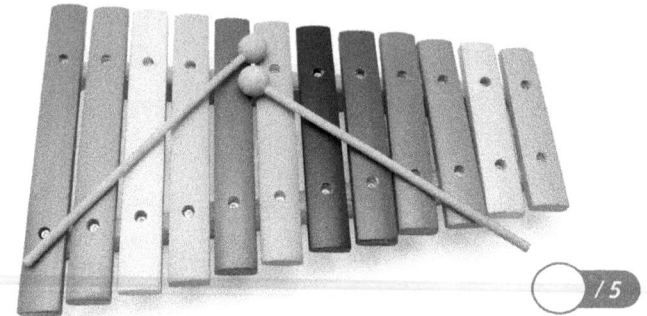

1 sword	axe	legend
2 robber	instructor	burglar
3 bargain	fashion	style
4 xylophone	drum	pianist
5 storm	damage	flood

/ 5

B Complete the sentences with these words.

> connection   diploma   leaflet   leather   lifejacket

1 Everyone in the boat was wearing a _____ .
2 Mike has a fast Internet _____ .
3 The salesperson gave me a _____ as I left the shop.
4 She got her _____ when she finished college.
5 These sandals are made of fine _____ .

/ 5

C Circle the correct words.

1 Most people feel stressed / terrified when they have a difficult problem.
2 Mike hurt his arm yesterday and today it feels very careless / sore.
3 Betty listens to soft / fair music when she wants to relax.
4 Don't be like Mark. He spent too much money and now he has receipts / debts.
5 Rob's mum told him to stop surfing / playing so many video games on the computer.

/ 5

D Match.

1 Pilots are trained in how to land	a some files from her computer.
2 Sheila forgot to delete	b the man who broke into Mary's house.
3 People who commit	c a plane correctly.
4 Louis told the judge that he didn't steal	d any money.
5 The police arrested	e crimes should receive some kind of punishment.

/ 5

E Complete the letter with these prepositions.

> about   for   for   in   into   on   out   over   through   with

Hi Stella,

How are you? I haven't talked to you in a while. I tried to call you last week, but I couldn't get (1) _____ . I decided to send you a letter instead and tell you about my summer.

Firstly, my family and I went to New Zealand for two weeks in June. It was my first time there. I was worried (2) _____ flying to a place so far away, but once we were in the air, I quickly got (3) _____ my fears. The place is very beautiful and so green. It was a little bit cold at times. There was definitely no need (4) _____ any summer clothes during our trip, as it's winter in New Zealand in June. We did many exciting things such as hiking across glaciers and camping in the countyside. I had an argument (5) _____ my parents about going abseiling. They said it's too dangerous and I would need training, so I didn't go in the end.

After returning from holiday, though, I decided to look (6) _____ abseiling a bit more. I found a training centre not far from my house. They had a summer training course (7) _____ special offer, so I decided to take it. I had a wonderful time and met lots of exciting people who love outdoor sports. A couple of people on the course even asked me if I wanted to start working (8) _____ with them. It's funny, actually. They said they've been going to a gym on my street (9) _____ ages. I didn't even know there was a gym on my street!

How's your job as a volunteer at the animal rescue centre? Have you succeeded (10) _____ helping lots of animals? I certainly hope so.

That's all for now. Talk to you soon,

Georgia

◯ / 10

Grammar

A Circle the correct answers.

1 Many cars are weighing / weigh about 1,000 kilos.
2 Sam has driven / has been driving his motorbike for three hours now.
3 Laura bought a boat because she moved / had moved to a house near the lake.
4 Marty won't sell / won't have sold his yacht by the end of the summer.
5 Jessica misses to walk / walking in the evenings with her friends.

◯ / 5

B Read the dialogue that two girls had yesterday and choose the correct answers.

Mary: I'm wearing a new dress today. Have you noticed?
Nancy: Yes, it looks great. Did you buy it yesterday?
Mary: Yes, I bought it from a shop near my house yesterday morning. We can go there together if you want.

1 Mary said that she _____ a new dress.
   a is wearing   b wears   c was wearing
2 Mary asked Nancy if she _____ her new dress.
   a noticed   b had noticed   c would notice
3 Nancy said that the dress _____ great.
   a looks   b looked   c had looked
4 Nancy asked if Mary had bought the dress _____ .
   a yesterday   b the day before   c that day
5 Mary said she and Nancy _____ go to the shop together.
   a could   b can   c should

◯ / 5

C Complete the dialogue with the causative.

Paul: Mimi, I (1) _____ (the car / wash) later today.

Mimi: Good idea! Are you going to (2) _____ (the inside / clean), too?

Paul: No, the inside's fine. Would you like to come along?

Mimi: Sorry, I have to go to the jewellery shop. I (3) _____ (a ring / fix) last week and it's ready now. Then I'm off to the hairdresser's to (4) _____ (my hair / do).

Paul: Sounds like you're quite busy, Mimi.

Mimi: Have you forgotten what today is, Paul? I'm going to the photographer's.

Paul: Oh right! You can't (5) _____ (your photo / take) without looking your best!

/ 5

D The words in bold are wrong. Write the correct words.

1 'Do you need help?' 'No, I **have to** do it.'   _____

2 Lizzy **can** read when she was 3 years old.   _____

3 **Must** I go to a university nearby or far away?   _____

4 You **don't have to** talk in the library. It's not allowed.   _____

5 He hasn't **be** able to eat all day.   _____

/ 5

E Complete the conditional sentences with the correct form of these words.

buy	decide	feel	go	not meet

1 If you don't come to my party, you _____ my friends.

2 I _____ a pair of skis if they weren't so expensive.

3 If I _____ to take up a new sport, it would be basketball.

4 If it hadn't snowed all night long, we _____ to the mountains yesterday.

5 _____ he _____ bad if he hadn't passed the test?

/ 5

F Choose the correct answers.

1 Expensive outfits _____ sold in this shop any more.
   a isn't
   b aren't
   c weren't

2 A concert has _____ in this theatre before.
   a being performed
   b performed
   c been performed

3 Can her new song _____ on the radio?
   a hear
   b heard
   c be heard

4 'We're going to be late.' 'Yes, if only we _____ earlier.'
   a leave
   b had left
   c have left

5 The teacher told the students to behave _____ .
   a herself
   b itself
   c themselves

/ 5

Reading

A Read this article about an extreme sport.

You probably already know about extreme sports such as paragliding, abseiling and bungee jumping. However, have you heard of a sport called BASE jumping? In some ways it's similar to the other three sports. It involves putting on a parachute and jumping off something very tall.

The letters B, A, S and E are for the four things which BASE jumpers jump off - buildings, antennas, spans (bridges) and the Earth itself in the form of a cliff or a mountain. After a BASE jumper has jumped from all four types, he or she can get a number, known as a 'BASE number'. The first number was given in 1981, and since then, over 1,300 BASE jumpers have been given numbers.

BASE jumping came from the extreme sport of skydiving. In skydiving, people jump out of aeroplanes and travel to the ground with a parachute. BASE jumpers, however, jump from places that are much closer to the Earth. BASE jumpers have much less time to prepare before they land. If they don't do everything correctly, the parachute may not open. They can also hit the side of the building or mountain they are jumping from. Skydivers always use two parachutes. If one doesn't open, the other one will. However, a BASE jump happens so fast that there isn't enough time for a second parachute to open.

A favourite place for BASE jumpers is the New River Gorge Bridge in Fayetteville, West Virginia. The bridge is 267 metres above the river. Once a year on a Saturday in October, the people of Fayetteville welcome BASE jumpers who jump from the bridge. During the six-hour period, about 450 people make a jump. Sometimes there are as many as 200,000 people watching, and they are almost as excited as the jumpers. It's definitely the most important day of the year in that small town!

Comprehension

B Choose the correct answers.

1 BASE jumping is _____ other extreme sports.
   a exactly the same as
   b similar to
   c completely different from

2 Who can get a BASE number?
   a someone who has jumped from a building
   b anyone who wants to do a jump
   c someone who has done all types of jumps

3 How are BASE jumping and skydiving different?
   a Skydivers jump from higher places.
   b BASE jumpers jump from higher places.
   c BASE jumpers jump from planes.

4 BASE jumpers have only one parachute because _____
   a two parachutes are too heavy.
   b they can fall faster with only one parachute.
   c they only have time to open one.

5 About _____ people jump in Fayetteville's annual BASE jumping event.
   a 267
   b 450
   c 200,000

/ 10

Writing

Write an article about mobile phones. Use this plan to help you.

Paragraph 1
Introduce the topic.
Talk about how much people use mobile phones these days and what they are used for.

Paragraph 2
Describe some advantages of having a mobile phone.
Explain why some people need mobile phones.

Paragraph 3
Describe some disadvantages of mobile phones.
Give one or more solutions for these problems.

Paragraph 4
Write a conclusion explaining your feelings about mobile phones.

/ 10

Total   / 80